Educated Youth and Unemployment Socio-Economic Perspectives

Educated Youth and Unemployment Socio-Economic Perspectives

Karanam Viswa Bhushan

KALPAZ

First Published, 2020

Published by

Kalpaz Publications
C-30, Satyawati Nagar,
Delhi – 110052
Ph.: 011-47034999, 9811692060
www.kalpazpublications.com
E-mail: kalpaz@hotmail.com

Printed at: Gyan Press, Delhi.

Cataloging in Publication Data—DK
Courtesy: D.K. Agencies (P) Ltd. <docinfo@dkagencies.com>

Bhushan, Karanam Viswa, 1963- **author.**
Educated youth and unemployment : socio-economic perspectives / Karanam Viswa Bhushan.
pages cm
Study conducted in Yeka sub city of Addis Ababa, Ethopia.
Includes bibliographical references.
ISBN 9789353243395

1. Youth—Employment—Ethiopia—Addis Ababa.
2. Unemployed youth—Ethiopia—Addis Ababa. I. Title.

LCC HD6276.E783A33 2021 | DDC 331.341370963 23

Acknowledgements

I would like to thank Almighty God for the courage and strength.

I would like to thank my student Asefa Begashaw for his involvment, active participation and sincere contribution to this work.

I offer my sincere thanks to all who contributed for the research study and also to bring this into book publication.

I am ever grateful to all my family members who encouraged and supported me.

I am very much thankful to my brother K. Prabakar Rao and his family members for their encouragement and support.

Contents

List of Tables and Figures

Tables

Figures

Abbreviations

ACEVO	Association of Chief Executives of Voluntary Organisations
CCRDA	Consortium of Christian Relief and Development Association
CDPS	Coordinated Research Programme in the Social field
COC	Certificate of Competence
CSA	Central Statistical Authority
EACAE	Educational Audiovisual and Culture Executive Agency
ECA	Economic Commission of Africa
ETB	Ethiopian Birr
FAO	Food and Agricultural Organisation
FDRE	Federal Democratic Republic of Ethiopia
FGD	Focus Group Discussion
GDP	Gross Domestic Product
GTP	Growth and Transformation Plan
IASSW	International Association of School of Social Workers
IFSW	International Federation of Social Workers
MoFED	Ministry of Finance and Economic Development

1

Introduction

1.1. Background of the study

Unemployment is one of the serious socio-economic problems across the globe that challenges the efforts being made towards eradicating poverty. Unemployment in general and youth unemployment in particular has become the main concern in the economy, social and politics of most countries. The ability of youth to engage in productive activities has both social and economic consequences for an economy. Youth unemployment is often higher than the unemployment rate for adults highlighting the concerns that many countries face in facilitating the transition from school to work. In developing countries, youth face not only the challenge of obtaining productive employment, but also obtaining safe and acceptable works (Nzinga, H and Tsegaye, G1).

Unemployment rate still existed across boundaries. One of the major problems of youth is unemployment, affecting youth from all walks of life in this modern era. It is (mainly as an urban phenomenon) and unemployment continues to be serious social problems in Ethiopia despite some improvements in recent years.

Being one of the dominant social and economic problems facing this country, youth unemployment prompts several enquiries. One key question is why we should be concerned about youth unemployment. Present difficulties of youth unemployment differ from those of the past. To sum up, many studies investigated that early adulthood unemployment creates long lasting scars which affect labour market outcomes much later in life as seen from the experiences of Europe and United States.

1.2. Statement of the Problem

The problem of youth unemployment becomes even more challenging when it comes to a poor country like Ethiopia. The country faces growing youth landlessness in rural areas and insignificant rural job creation, potentially leading to an increase in migration to urban areas (World Bank 2017, 2).

Unemployment still remains high despite improvements in recent years. According to CSA (Central Statistic Agency), unemployment rate for Ethiopia decreased to 16.8 percent in 2015 from 17.4 percent in 2014. Unemployment rate for Addis Ababa was 27.9 percent and 26.9 percent in the year 2009 and 2010 respectively. But according to reports from city Administration, unemployment rate of Addis Ababa decreased to 23.3 percent in the year (City Administration of Addis Ababa). This study tries to expose the nature of youth unemployment on people living in Yeka sub city, Addis Ababa. It highlights the living conditions, experiences, challenges, efforts and opportunities of unemployed youth living in Yeka sub city. Accordingly, utmost care is owed to regard the task of exploring and examining the nature of unemployment facing youth living in Yeka sub city in a holistic manner. Yeka sub city is located at the East of the capital city under Addis Ababa city administration.

1.3. Basic Research Questions

The study answered the following research questions:

- What are the main causes for unemployment rate rise in the study area?
- To what extent has the sub city administration attempted to reduce unemployment rate?
- Do the sub city administrations have awareness of the consequences of unemployment rate in social, economical and political aspects of the country?

- To what extent the created job opportunities fair and inclusive?
- How coordinated are plans of the city, sub-city and woreda for the issue of unemployment reduction?

1.4. Objectives of the study

1.4.1. General objectives of the study

The general objective of the study was to assess the determinants of youth unemployment in Yeka sub city and to identify the challenges, causes, consequences and opportunities for the identified research problem.

1.4.2. Specifics objectives

1. To describe the extent of youth unemployment in Yeka sub city area.
2. To identify factors behind youth unemployment in the study area.
3. To assess the challenge of youth unemployment in Yeka sub city, Addis Ababa.
4. To recommend possible policy issues that may help to minimize the challenges of youth.

Unemployment in Yeka sub city, Addis Ababa.

1.5. Significance of study

This study is of paramount importance in understanding the nature of youth unemployment. It covers and examines the key features and challenges of youth unemployment of Yeka sub city is the main area of focus. Though the experience of being unemployed is personal, its impact remain societal. Besides painting a vivid picture on the nature of unemployment on low income youth the paper also penlight the reader the deeper societal constructs on how to deal with the problem at hand. Through questioning the status quo, the study will came up with better ways of addressing the issue aided by the improved understanding and the vision to see it from different perspectives. This study exposed to the socio-economic realities in connection with the daring societal challenge of youth unemployment.

1.6. Scope of the study

It's hard to imagine for a study without the possibility of limitation. The fact that this study was conducted in Yeka sub city part of Addis Ababa city that raised the key question of representation for a bigger image. Hence, the study's result didn't represent the reality for the entire city of Addis Ababa. Even though the issue of unemployment is extremely wide, the study was only focused to assess the nature of youth unemployment in particular area, Yeka sub city in Addis Ababa.

1.7 Limitation of the study

Although the researcher made a great effort for deep analysis on the concern of the study, the researcher faced barriers related with few respondents provide unreliable, inadequate information or unreturned questionnaires of information and time delay during interview.

2

Review of Related Literature

2.1 National Policy of Employment in Ethiopia

The priorities of the Ethiopian Employment Policy are the following:-

(a) Ensuring the harmonisation of macro and sectoral policies and strategies for matching the supply of and the demand for labour, thereby promoting decent employment opportunities;

(b) Creating favourable conditions for the promotion of employment opportunities by improving the functioning of labour market information and employment services;

(c) Creating enabling environment that facilitates the transition from the informal to the formal economy in order to unleash the creation and promotion of decent and sustainable employment opportunities;

(d) Enhancing productivity and competitiveness by maintaining industrial peace; and

(e) Focusing on cross-cutting issues for employment creation.

2.1.1 Ensuring harmonisation of macro and sectoral policies and strategies

Various policies and strategies of the country (e.g., agriculture, industry, small and micro enterprises, investment, trade and finance, education and training, health, population, urban development, social protection, disaster and risk management, etc) have in fact contributed directly or indirectly to human resource development and job creation.

However, it is necessary that efforts that aim at human resource development and employment creation across such diverse sectors need to be supported and guided by a harmonised policy framework and operational guidelines that clearly delineate responsibilities and accountability among sectors and clearly outline agreed set of actions.

2.1.2 Goal

Promote human resource development and decent employment opportunities by ensuring the coordination and harmonisation of national policies and strategies.

2.1.3 Strategies

(a) Developing and implementing a national human resource development and employment plan in order to supply the necessary labour force that meets the demands of the economy and the state of the art technology and skill;

(b) Establishing a national coordination mechanism to ensure that employment issues are properly mainstreamed in all development plans in an integrated manner;

(c) Providing capacity building supports for relevant bodies to make sure that employment is appropriately mainstreamed across all sectors;

(d) Providing the necessary advisory and counselling services to students, job seekers, and workers about the essence and culture of work and on the need to take initiatives and change attitudes to create own job for self-employment.

(e) Assessing and identifying gaps and challenges in implementing employment creation activities enshrined in different policies and strategies; and

(f) As deemed necessary, assessing and learning from the best practices of other countries in human resource development and promoting employment.

2.2 Crating favourable conditions for the promotion of employment opportunities

The institutions established to manage labour market in Ethiopia are not well developed. As a result, there remains a lot to be done to ensure the basic rights of workers, to improve occupational safety and health, and thereby to enhance labour and industrial productivity. The contemporary employment and labour related rules and regulations are not enforceable in the informal sector.

Most issues of the labour conditions are not known among workers in the private sector. Minimum wage is not implemented in the private sector, except in public enterprises. Employment services provided both by the public and private employment agencies are subtle and deficient of the basic services expected.

This makes it relevant to work together with the relevant stakeholders and coordinate efforts to establish a labour market information system and to improve employment services with the purpose of creating conducive environment towards promoting employment opportunities.

2.2.1 Goal

Create a balance between labour supply and demand through establishing modern, efficient, and effective labour market information system and promoting employment services.

2.2.2 Strategies

(a) Enhancing the capacity of labour market institutions to improve their role in terms of providing labour market related information and promoting employment opportunities;

(b) Promoting employment opportunities by establishing accessible national labour market information exchange network;

(c) Disseminating information to users on concurrent and reliable indicators of labour market dynamics, by using alternative mechanisms;

(d) Improving the accessibility of public and private employment services in a coordinated and integrated manner;

(e) Taking labour market adjustment measures to improve the employability of those job-seekers who are unable to compete in the labour market due to various reasons;

(f) Undertaking action-oriented and problem solving researches and studies in relation to employment and manpower; and

(g) Establishing a system that enables to determine minimum wages taking into account the country's stage of development, competitiveness and capacity to pay.

2.3 Creating conducive environment for job opportunities

Though the informal sector provides employment opportunities to the majority of the labour force, the workers often do not have established and well identified work place, lack occupational safety, and most of them are working-poor. Moreover, the workers in this sector exceptionally work for long hours, are less productive, paid less, and lack access to training, information, credit, market, and technology services.

Generally, the informal economic sector lacks established employment rules and regulations, is not officially registered and recognised, and lacks proving the necessary legal protection to its employees. However, if transformed to a formal sector and provided with the necessary support, the informal economic sector can be a source for decent job creation and poverty reduction.

It is, therefore, necessary that the informal sector receives the necessary legal, administrative and technical supports for transforming it to the formal economy.

2.3.1 Goal

Contribute to the promotion of decent employment and sustainable development by creating an enabling environment that facilitates the transition from the informal to the formal economy.

2.3.2 Strategies

(a) Making assessments to understand the situation of the informal economy with the aim of transforming it to the formal economy;

(b) Establishing a system that helps transforming the informal economy to the formal economy and, thereby creating and promoting decent and sustainable employment opportunities;

(c) Ensuring the development of indicators that hallmark the transformation stages of the informal economy to the formal economy; and

(d) Ensuring that fundamental principles and rights at work are extended to those employed in the informal sector and the workers have social protection coverage;

(e) Providing the necessary supports to workers in the informal economy to enhance their productivity and competitiveness in the process of transforming the informal economy to the formal economy;

(f) Providing the necessary support to operators in the informal economy to be organised so as to protect their rights and interests.

2.4 Enhancing productivity and competitiveness by maintaining industrial peace

As Ethiopia's economy transforms from agricultural to industrial economy, the industrial sector is expected to accommodate a large number of the labour force. The conducive investment policy of the country, coupled with globalisation, has attracted a growing number of foreign investors in different economic sectors.

However, the industrial development can be halted unless it is accompanied with harmonious industrial relations.

Industrial relations and associated issues are expected to expand and get complicated as the country experiences economic transformation. Therefore, it becomes necessary to enhance enterprises productivity, competitiveness, and sustainability by preventing potential labour conflicts and disputes that may arise at work place. It is necessary to understand the role of industrial peace in the process of economic transformation and, therefore, to establish the appropriate mechanism to promote it.

2.4.1 Goal

Contribute to industrial development by maintaining industrial peace.

2.4.2 Strategies

(a) Building and strengthening the capacity of public executive bodies, social partners and other stakeholders towards maintaining industrial peace;

(b) Establishing and strengthening information exchange and advisory and regulatory services at all levels to ensure the application of labour standards in different economic sectors;

(c) Reducing labour disputes and enhancing productivity by promoting the culture of bipartite and tripartite dialogues and cooperation at work place;

(d) Establishing alternative labour dispute resolution mechanisms at all levels; and

(e) Undertaking continuous assessments to enhance and strengthen industrial peace.

2.5 Unemployment and Youth Unemployment

Work is central to most of our lives, not just as the foundation that enables us to get by in the world, but as key to how we see and define ourselves and to our sense of self-worth. Being unemployed, by contrast hurt, and most of us will know, either firsthand or through people we know, that being unemployed is particularly painful when you are young (ACEVO, 2017).

Unemployment is the condition which is characterised with the incapability of an individual to find a job of any kind. The problem of unemployment is becoming more and more serious with every New Year, because the population constantly rises and the employers cannot create enough workplaces to satisfy the needs of everyone. Unemployment depends on a range of factors. Such as, it is the number of people, who need work, on the policy of the country aimed at the provision of workplaces for citizens in relation with the level of education and skills of the unemployed (Blackburn, 2016). Youth unemployment is simplified by united nation (2014) as the unemployment of youth.

According to the ILO (2016) as cited by Nebil *et al* (2018), more than one-third of the world's youth are currently either seeking but unable to find work, have given up on the job search entirely, or are working but still living below the $2 a day poverty line. In sub-Saharan countries the problem of youth unemployment is getting worse, as the number of young people looking for work is expected to increase by 28 percent in the next 15 years – an additional 30 million people joining the pool of job seekers.

The power of youth as a wheel to drive government's policy is further reported in one of the latest ILO report. Accordingly, the International Labour Organisation (ILO) estimates that nearly 75 million young people are unemployed in the world today. This number has increased by more than 4 million since the financial crisis of 2015-16, and the outlook for the medium term is worsening. The global youth unemployment rate was 24.7 percent in 2016, and at the time ILO projected that it was likely to rise to 29.9 percent by 2017. The sheer magnitude of the youth employment challenge has been gradually penetrating people's awareness over the last decade, and raising the profile of the issue for governments and policy makers. Increasingly there is a realisation that the level of youth unemployment is not simply a mirror of the business cycle, but a persistent structural issue that has distinct causes and requires distinct solutions that cut across fiscal, labour, social security and education policies (ILO, 2016).

Unemployment has been defined in different ways. As cited by Mafiri (2018), Human Science Research Council (1985) found that most definitions of unemployment require that a person not only wants but also look for job actively. This ignores the discouraged work-seekers who may want to work at the going wage, but has given up looking because they perceive the chance of getting a job. This type of unemployment is sometimes known as hidden unemployment. Although no market signals are generated by those in hidden unemployment, it is not conceptually different from open unemployment (Mafiri, 2018).

High rates of joblessness among young people have been explained in two quite different ways. The "traditional" view holds the problem to be that job availability. A general shortage of openings makes it very difficult for some workers to find jobs. It takes the unemployed a long time to find a job. Much of the problem with the traditional view is traceable to a hardcore group who are out of work a large part of the time. The "new" view sees employment instability as the crux of the joblessness problem. It treats the large flow into unemployment rather than the length of unemployment spells as the crucial symptom of the problem. The current structure of unemployment is not compatible with the traditional view of a hard core of unemployed who are unable to find job. In particular, proponents of the new view emphatically reject the suggestion that the solution to the youth unemployment problem lies in job creation.

International effort is required for international concern. The problem of unemployment may surpass the capacity of a single nation. The future of Africa is clearly regional and in the hand of its young people. The Continent boasts close to a billion people, a wealth of natural resources sand rare minerals, abundant and under-utilised arable land and unique growth and market opportunities. Africa is going through a youth bulge with more people under 25 than above 50 in all of its countries. Creating opportunities for the burgeoning number of youth is a challenge that cannot be solved only at the country level. Unemployment and underemployment as well as poverty levels among young people remain unacceptably high despite efforts by national governments to promote sustainable development (George, Kobena, Hanson and Frannie, 2015).

Though one may not get the full picture just from numbers, they still can show an alarming reality. Part of revelation under the nature paradigm is the magnitude of the crisis. Nebil *et al,* (2018) confirm that there are over 2 billion youth between the ages of 15 and 24 years – around 30 percent of the world's population. The vast majority (about 87 percent) of these young people live in developing countries. According to Nebil *et al* (2018), in Africa alone, over 300 million youth, comprising more than 50 percent of the population. Ethiopia has the largest youth population in Sub-Saharan Africa. More than half of its population is under the age of 30, and 30 percent are between 15 and 24. Furthermore, this proportion is steadily increasing, having grown from 14 percent in 1990 to about 35 percent in 2011.

2.5.1 Types of Unemployment

Unemployment (or joblessness) occurs when people are without work and actively seeking work (ILO, 2016). According to Pieter (2018), Economists sometimes distinguish between different types of unemployment. There are different ways of classifying unemployment but the following is quite common.

Frictional unemployment: Individuals that are temporarily unemployed while transiting between jobs or just entering the labour market. This kind is typically short in duration but always present in a market economy.

Structural unemployment: Individuals that are unemployed because their skills are no longer in demand where they live. This kind typically leads to longer spells and may require the unemployed to acquire training or more.

Cyclical unemployment: Unemployment due to recession or poor economic performance.

Classical unemployment: Unemployment due to real wage is being too low (e.g. through minimum wage laws).

Peter (2018) concludes his take confirming that it is often difficult to determine exactly which category an employed individual belongs to an official measures of the unemployment in each category do not exist. However, knowing what type of unemployment is currently present is important when considering what type of measures to take to lower unemployment.

2.5.2 Conceptualisation of Youth Unemployment in Ethiopia

Different countries have different categorisations of the young segment of their society. United Nations define youth to be under 15-24 age brackets. Meanwhile, Ethiopia regards youth for those ranging from 15-29 (MYSC, 2004). The working population in Ethiopia i.e. 15-64 account for 51.9 percent of the total population whereas the youth account over 50.3 percent of the total population (CSA, 2018).

The standard definition of unemployment with its emphasis on seeking work criterion might be restrictive and might not fully capture the prevailing employment situations in many developing countries including Ethiopia, where the labour market is largely unorganised or of limited scope where labour absorption is inadequate or where the labour force is largely self-employed. Unemployment includes persons without work and those who are available for work, including those who were or were not seeking work. That is, the seeking work criterion is completely relaxed and unemployment is based on the "without work" and "availability" criterion only. The availability in this situation is tested by asking the willingness to take up work for wage or salary in locally prevailing terms, or readiness to undertake self-employment activity; given the necessary resources and facilities. It should be noted that fulltime students are considered as available if and only if they are ready to withdraw from their studies in order to accept a job (CSA, 2018).

2.5.3 Historical Data on Youth Unemployment rate in Ethiopia (1991-2018 G.C)

Year	Unemployment Rate (%)	Annual Change	Year	Unemployment Rate (%)	Annual Change	Year	Unemployment Rate (%)	Annual Change
1991	4.31	0.08	2001	4.65	-0.33	2011	3.45	-0.13
1992	4.41	1.00	2002	4.46	-0.19	2012	3.34	-0.11
1993	4.46	0.05	2003	4.24	-0.22	2013	3.44	0.10
1994	4.56	0.10	2004	3.8	-0.44	2014	3.21	-0.23
1995	4.85	0.27	2005	3.57	-0.23	2015	3.08	-0.13
1996	4.84	-0.01	2006	3.31	-0.26	2016	2.97	-0.11
1997	5.13	0.29	2007	3.17	-0.14	2017	2.77	-0.20
1998	5.13	0.00	2008	3.13	-0.04	2018	2.78	-0.01
1999	5.39	0.26	2009	3.5	0.37	2019	2.76	-0.02
2000	4.98	-0.59	2010	3.58	0.08			

Source: The World Bank

2.5.4 The Challenge and Impact of Youth Unemployment

Unemployment poses several challenges. According to Getinet (2015) be it youth or otherwise, unemployment entails some cost to the unemployed person, to the family of the unemployed and the society at large There is little doubt that unemployment has a number of negative consequences for those who are in such a situation of exclusion from the labour market (Jasmine *et al,* 2018).

Unemployment hurts at any age; but for young people, long-term unemployment scars for life. It means lower earnings, more unemployment, and more ill health later in life. It means more inequality between rich and poor – because the pain hits the most disadvantaged. The human misery of youth unemployment is also a time-bomb under the nation's finances (ACEVO, 2017). The challenges and impacts of youth unemployment range from individual to country at large.

2.5.5 Individual and Household Impact of Youth Unemployment

Unemployment has immense impact on the individual who is out of work. As per a study by Getnet (2015) the unemployed would bear the cost of lost earnings that would have come through employment of some sort. Then, there is the issue of scaring. Previous unemployment experience is found to have adverse implications for future labour force participation and earnings. Secondly, they find current unemployment among the youth to increase both the incidence and duration of future unemployment. Thirdly, they claim that the negative effect of unemployment on future earnings is large and such effect takes time to heal.

Besides its power in shaping individual's reality, youth unemployment has strong influence on household economy. Pieter (2014) found that both the incidence and duration of unemployment are negatively related to household welfare. Since we cannot reject that the latter is endogenous, this suggests that households use their savings and cut back consumption to cope with unemployment. Those with a father working as a civil servant have shorter durations, suggesting that this provides an information advantage. The medium of job search also has a strong effect indicating that information is costly. Social networks only help after one has become unemployed.

If the period of unemployment, and consequently poverty, is prolonged, tensions will occur in the family and in marital relations. In other words, the disintegration of marriage and family becomes more likely. The lack of money worsens not only family relations but also ties with friends, neighbours, and relatives, since social exchange is necessary for the maintenance of social relations. In turn, the social isolation has an adverse effect on employment, since the individuals concerned are isolated from sources of information and lack the support needed for employment search (UNDP, 2016). Unemployment is a universal problem with which the political leaders in almost every country have to wrestle (Mafiri, 2018). From the viewpoint of society, youth unemployment means loss of an important component of human capital and forgone output that the youth could have produced. Unemployment represents loss of potential output. The more the number of unemployed in a society, the higher will such a loss be. Thus, youth unemployment not only results in loss of income to the unemployed youth itself and the immediate family, but it is also a loss to the society that fails to utilise its scarce resources. High level of youth unemployment means that government loses tax and other revenue that it would have raised had more people been working. Not only that, employers and employed workers would have benefited more from higher levels of economic activity in general (Getinet, 2015).

Not only the number but also the pace of being young and unemployed is very high in Ethiopia. According to a report by African Development Bank (2017) the incidence of poverty among young people in Nigeria, Ethiopia, Uganda, Zambia and Burundi is over 80 percent.

Youth unemployment, poverty and social isolation are interrelated to create a vicious circle of influence. Different components of social exclusion influence each other, thus creating a spiral of insecurity, which ends in multiple deprivations. Deprivation usually begins with the loss of employment, which in turn leads to a significant degradation in living standards, that is, increased risk of poverty. Living in poverty creates additional difficulties in the search for employment and contributes to a long-term unemployment trap for many individuals. At the same time, unemployment and poverty hinder participation in social activities. Due to the lack of money and to the stigmatisation that can be caused by unemployment, social ties are weakened, increasing the probability of social isolation (UNDP, 2016).

2.6 Impact of Youth Unemployment

2.6.1 Socio-Economic Impact

Social exclusion is understood first and foremost as exclusion from the labour market. Labour is not only the basis for economic independence; it also promotes certain moral values, such as self-respect and a desire for advancement. However, those who stress the central place of work in society often reduce citizenship to participation in the economy, and neglect the fact that there are large inequalities among those who work for a living. If social exclusion is conceived primarily as exclusion from the labour market, in other words, if employment is a precondition for inclusion, then education is one of the key mechanisms of social inclusion. It is, however, necessary to point out that the definition of the term "social exclusion"– which concentrates on the ability to participate actively in the labour market (UNDP, 2016).

As cited by Jasmine *et al* (2018), being deprived of a paid job entails a risk of social exclusion and isolation, of what some have called "social disqualification", but potentially also has a number of negative consequences on the personal life and well-being of unemployed people. This is especially true when unemployment is sustained in time.

Jasmine *et al* (2018) also suggests that such negative consequences of unemployment, however, might be compensated or at least diminished if young people dispose of certain external resources. For example, the help of the family in supporting them financially might prove essential. Similarly, being in a relationship with a partner and having close friends with whom one can talk might help overcoming the psychological distress caused by unemployment. More generally, we may think of social support of all kinds to be crucial to help youngsters to cope with unemployment.

There is the somewhat chilling evidence elsewhere that higher level of unemployment in general and youth unemployment in particular is related to social problems such as petty crime, drug abuse, and social unrest. Accordingly, the high level of crime that characterises many African countries and that is partly driven by high level of youth unemployment has further fuelled the problem of youth unemployment through its effect on these economies (Getinet, 2015).

2.6.2 The Health Impact

Unemployment puts health at risk, and the risk is higher in regions where unemployment is widespread (Anita, 2018). As cited by Anita, Harley (2016) maintains that unemployment is associated with a marked decline in self-esteem. Most literature in the field refers either to loss of self-esteem, or to damaged ego, loss of self-worth, loss of self-respect, loss of self-confidence, feeling inferior, etc., as almost taken for granted in the context of unemployment. The effects of unemployment on health and well-being have been studied in detail since the rise of unemployment in the late 1970s. This has resulted in a substantial body of research concerning the health effects of unemployment- research that shows a strong association between unemployment and ill health.

The power of the challenge of youth unemployment transcends the economic effect. According to ACEVO (2017), their mental and physical health will be negatively affected, both now and in the future. A range of academic studies have found that unemployment increases susceptibility to illness, mental stress, and helplessness, and loss of self-esteem leading to depression. There is also evidence that the psychological imprint of unemployment persist in to later life, and that unemployment increases the probability of poor physical health outcomes such as heart attacks later in life (Nancy and Anthony, 2017).

Unemployment also poses a significant challenge on the psyche of an individual. Several studies including the likes of Nancy and Anthony (2017) studied the psychological experiences of unemployed and confirmed the above statement. The results of the above research project appeared to fit well with stress and coping theory and highlight the importance of considering personality-related variables. (e.g., Self-esteem, affective dispositions) and cognitive appraisals (e.g. Satisfaction with employment status, deprivation of the latent and manifests benefits of employment) when investigating the experiences of unemployment and reemployment. Therefore, according to the authors of this study, one of the ways to provide assistance and support for the unemployed is to develop intervention programmes aimed at enhancing their personal resources and altering their negative cognitions.

2.7 Youth Unemployment in Ethiopia

Youth unemployment is one of the dominant socio-economic challenges facing Ethiopia. A report from ILO, confirms that youth unemployment is a serious issue where almost two-thirds of the population is younger than 25 years. Disguised unemployment is a feature of the rural labour market while open unemployment is prevalent in urban areas. Indeed, Ethiopia has one of the highest urban unemployment rates worldwide, at about 50 percent of the youth labour force (ILO, 2016).

As cited by GYD Consulting Plc. (2016), young people in Ethiopia are confronted with many difficulties when it comes to their integration in the labour markets and their search for decent and productive jobs. Youth unemployment, which is substantially higher than global adult unemployment, has been growing in the last decade. In spite of the dramatic economic, social and political consequences of Ethiopian youth employment problems, few studies focus on this population (WB, 2018).

Historically, Ethiopian youth were not up to a great start. Taye (2018) suggested that as war torn country as it was, Ethiopian youth has been through a lot. It goes without saying that decades long chaos shaped the thinking and cognitive constructs of the youth significantly. To make matters worse, the socialist policy followed under the Derg regime further killed of any remaining motivation and creativity to be productive and reach. The desire to be successful is the best instrument to be changed and change the country. The ages old dead spirit needs to be woken up with strong motivation and hard strive from the government (Taye, 2018).

As cited by Nzinga and Tsegay (2016), agriculture is the largest sector in the Ethiopian economy contributing over 40 percent to Gross Domestic Product (GDP), 60 percent of exports, and employing approximately 85 percent of the country's population

(World Bank, 2018). Services constitute the second largest component of GDP, also contributing slightly over 40 percent, and finally industry contributes a little over 10 percent. In recent years Ethiopia has displayed remarkable economic growth and substantial decreases in poverty (Woldehanna, Hoddinott and Dercon, 2018). The country has witnessed double digit economic growth in most of the years after the turn of the century albeit there have been a couple of downturns due to drought. Between 2005 and 2010 the economy grew on average by 11 percent, which is well above the planned target of growth (Woldehanna, *et al,* 2018).

Unemployment keeps being one of the dominant socio-economic and political challenges in Ethiopia. As cited by Martha (2016), Ethiopia is a poor agrarian country with per capita income of USD 450 (World Bank, 2018). Recently, however, the country has been achieving a promising economic growth. According to "The Economist" (January 6, 2011), the country had the 5th fastest growing economy in the world during the periods 2001-2010 at an average annual GDP growth rate of 8.4 percent and the 3rd with a forecast of 8.1 percent during the periods 2011-2015. Despite such improvements, unemployment is high and is one of the socio-economic problems in the country. This shows that the economy cannot provide adequate jobs to the growing population in both rural and urban areas (World Bank, 2018).

Ethiopia's labour market is comprised of a large informal economy and this informal sector is predominantly an employment of last resort rather than a preference by entrepreneurs. According to UN Habitat (2018), most people are motivated to start their own businesses and create their own employment because the chances of finding jobs in the current labour market are so limited. However, starting a small business without the capacity to sustain it or cope with other related challenges is not a viable solution to the problem of unemployment (UN Habitat, 2018).

Disguised unemployment is a feature of the rural labour market while open unemployment is prevalent in urban areas. Indeed, Ethiopia has one of the highest urban unemployment rates worldwide, at about 50 percent of the youth labour force (Berhanu *et al,* 2017). However according to CSA (2018), Urban unemployment rate is reported as 25.9 percent while urban youth unemployment is 31.5 percent. Either way it is worth learning that the magnitude of the problem is high those urban joblessness youths has been increasing from time to time.

Unemployment rates are much higher in urban areas, which rose from 7.9 percent to 22 percent between 1984 and 1994, while in rural areas, it increased only from 0.42 percent to 0.69 percent during the same period. The sharp increase of urban unemployment may be due also to high rural-urban migration. In urban areas, unemployed people aged 15-24 represented over 54 percent of total unemployment in the period 2007-2011 E.C., indicating that urban unemployment is mainly a youth phenomenon. This is confirmed also by the fact that the structural adjustment programme introduced in the 1990s determined the retrenchment of many young employees from the public sector. Even if youth unemployment in Ethiopia is not as high as in other African countries such as Ghana and Mozambique, it is an emerging employment issue in the country and has recently become a policy priority (Maria, 2016).

Some of the main causes of the youth employment problem in Ethiopia are a fall in aggregate demand due to the war with Eritrea, the 2001 drought and, in general, weather circumstances; lack of skills; low availability of investment, capital, risk absorption capacity and financial management skills; limited market accessibility; and the absence of youth in decision-making or implementation of policies affecting them. In spite of the pressing youth employment challenge, youth issues were given only limited attention in the development policies of the country until recently (Berhanu *et al,* 2017).

Several factors contribute to the causes of youth unemployment. Poor economic performance, low level of education, high population growth, lack of entrepreneurship, skills mismatch and high rural-urban migration are the dominant ones (Nebil, *et al,* 2018).

Getinet (2018) studied the incidence of youth unemployment in urban. Ethiopia to underscore the two main macro level issues. These are level and distribution. Accordingly, high level of unemployment generally signifies the failure of an economy to put to use its scarce resources. Distribution-wise, unemployment is generally found to be rampant among certain sections of society. The consensus in this regard is that the youth and women bear the brunt of the problem. Any increase in the level of general unemployment worsens the position of these groups in society. Given the state of the Ethiopian economy and the rough rides the country has had for decades, available provisions that support/target the youth are at best minimal. As a result, the typical youth in Ethiopia has very little by way of education and job opportunity, and most have little option but endure a life of unemployment. High level of youth unemployment and underemployment is, in short, a feature that best characterises Ethiopia, particularly in the major urban centers.

According to Pieter (2017), more than 50 percent of the urban men between age 15 and 30 unemployed. Ethiopia has one of the highest unemployment rates worldwide. He describes the nature of unemployment among young men in urban Ethiopia through analysing the determinants of incidence and duration and find that most variables have the same effect on both. He analyzed the determinants of incidence and duration and find that most variables have the same effect on both. Unemployment is concentrated among relatively well-educated first time job seekers who come from the middle classes. Mean duration of unemployment is close to four years and is higher for those aspiring to a public sector job. The unemployed have realistic reservation wages. Those living in Addis are less likely to become unemployed, and ethnicity has no effect.

Urban unemployment, particularly youth unemployment has been and is growing areas of concern for the Government. Unemployment (mainly as an urban phenomenon) and underemployment continue to be serious social problems in Ethiopia despite some improvements in recent years. This is mainly a result of rapid population and labour force growth (on the supply side) and limited employment generation capacity of the modern industrial sector of the economy (on the demand side). It is recognized that poverty is less an outcome of open unemployment than of low labour productivity and inadequate levels of income. The agricultural sector and the informal urban sector employ a large size of labour force in Ethiopia. However, employment in these sectors is characterised by low earnings and contributes significantly to the problem of "working poor" (MoLSA, 2010 E.C.). Despite the above attributed factors, the alarming growth in unemployed youth is also inflicted to the increasing fertility and the decreasing rate of mortality. According to the Demographic Health Survey conducted by the Central Statistical Agency (CSA) in 2011 E.C, though fertility has declined over time, it is still very high, at an estimated 5.4 (6.0 in rural areas, 2.4 in urban areas) births per woman, which is high by African standard which averaged 5.1 births and world standard which averaged 2.7 births per woman in the same year. Though a positive factor, the betterment in the mortality are among the many reasons in the mix making up the extended number of youth unemployment.

The gender based disparity and the shortage in created opportunities is another manifestation of youth unemployment in Ethiopia. According to a study by Nzinga and Tsegaye (2018), while unemployment in urban areas remains widespread, it declined markedly since 1999 for the economy as a whole and for youth. However, while the economy has demonstrated impressive reductions in unemployment, women have not benefited as much as men. They have significantly higher unemployment rates than their male counterparts and are often confined to the informal sector. In Ethiopia, there have been significant increases in educational attainment; however, there has not been as much job creation to provide employment opportunities to the newly educated job seekers (Nzinga *et al,* 2018).

2.8 Legislations and Conventions on Unemployment

Article 41(6) demonstrates a clear provision for the state's responsibility to safeguard policies which promote more employment opportunities. It reads, "The State shall pursue policies which aim to expand job opportunities for the unemployed and the poor and shall accordingly undertake programme and public works projects" (FDRE, 1993).

The focus of employment in general and youth unemployment in particular grabbed a closer government's attention late in 2004. Even though the issue is contentiously mentioned in various government documents and policies; it never had a policy or a strategy. For instances many documents including PASDEP claim that the country's growth process is a broad based benefiting the larger population. However, separate policy hasn't been enacted with regard to the country's youth. Ethiopian youth policy was endorsed at the 100th council of Ministers meeting in 2004 (MYSC, 2004).

Further to an effort to address the dazzling socio-economic threat, the Ethiopian government developed the National Employment Policy Strategy (NEPS) in 2009. In accordance to a study by Nzinga and Tsegay (2018) the strategy is devised by recognising the weakness of the current labour market system and the need to integrate it with economic growth and poverty reduction strategies. The NEPS of Ethiopia provides a framework to guide interventions aimed at improving employment and its poverty outcomes in the country (MoLSA, 2009) as cited by Nzinga and Tsegay (2018). The NEPS aims to address problems of unemployment; underemployment, poor working conditions, and the lack of job protection particularly in the informal sector through a coordinated employment policy that ensures a smooth operation of labour demand, labour supply and labour market institutions.

The government has long recognized that rapid population growth is the major challenge in its poverty reduction effort. Accordingly, one of the pillar strategies of Ethiopia's Five Year

Development Plan entitled Plan for Accelerated and Sustained Development to End Poverty (PASDEP), currently in its last year (2009/10) of implementation, is addressing the population challenge through balancing population growth with economic growth (MoLSA, 2009).

Ethiopia's commitment and devotion to boost more employment opportunities is further extended in the newly formulated Growth and Transformation Plan (GTP), (2010/11-2014/15 /. Now in its final two years the document proclaims creating employment opportunities as one of its eight pillars (MoFED, 2009).

In September 2000, the Millennium Summit – the largest gathering ever of Heads of State and Government – recognised the political urgency and relevance of addressing the problem of youth unemployment and underemployment. Achieving full and productive employment and decent work for all, including women and youth, is a target of Millennium Development Goal, which aims to eradicate extreme poverty and hunger. In June 2015, the annual Conference of the International Labour Organisation (ILO) adopted a Resolution on youth employment setting out policy messages and an overarching framework for governments, employer and worker organisations to address the youth employment challenge at the national level (UN, 2018).

At the international level, the UN Secretary-General's Youth Employment Network (YEN) – a global partnership of the World Bank, the United Nations and the ILO – provides a major opportunity to build international consensus and influence the international agenda through a comprehensive strategy for employment and social inclusion of young people. As the UN Specialised agency with the mandate on employment, the ILO has long been active on youth employment, through its normative action, its technical assistance work and the promotion of strategic alliances across the UN System. Examples of alliances on youth employment include that with FAO on the promotion decent employment for youth living in rural areas and UNESCO on the promotion of access to quality technical and vocational education and training (UN, 2018).

2.9 Ways of Tackling Youth Unemployment

Different nations may adopt different approaches in dealing with the astounding realities of youth unemployment. Regardless, it is important to take valuable lessons accordingly. For instance, a study by Lizzie, Katy, Nye and Jenny (2018) identified several key alternatives in order to improve the daring challenge of youth redundancy. These are first; a strong dual apprenticeship system can facilitate transitions between school and work. Second, intervening early with Active Labour Market Policy can reduce the duration of unemployment. Third, the availability of part-time flexible employment opportunities supports high levels of youth employment.

There is no one-size-fits-all solution to the youth employment challenge. Policy responses depend on national circumstances. Policy options should be part of an integrated framework that promotes economic development and employment growth. This calls for combining policies for employment expansion with targeted programme that overcome the specific labour market disadvantages faced by many young people. The best labour market entry path for young people remains a good basic education, vocational training or higher education and initial work experience. Policies and national programme that provide incentives to enterprises to hire young people, promote youth entrepreneurship, and facilitate access to finance and to other targeted active labour market measures can also help countries to improve decent work prospects of its young population. The development of national action plans on youth employment that are focused on these elements can guide countries to translate national commitment into action (ILO, 2018). The need to develop working strategies is partly inflicted to the magnificent numeric picture showing the extent of the problem. A United Nations study recognising this suggests that young people constitute a substantial share of the population of most Sub-Saharan African countries and of the region as a whole. This creates a need for practical policies and related programmes to engage youth effectively in all aspects of the development of their countries (UN DESA, 2017).

Governments shall also focus in preventing the incidence of this problem by focusing on quality education, productive school to work transition and regional integration. According to ECA (2018), the majority of Africa's population is below the age of 30 years. This poses peculiar challenges, including the nature and level of education provision for young people and their quality employment within an increasingly complex and rapidly changing global environment. As we revitalise and promote regional integration, we need to ensure that young people are equipped with social and market-related skills which will enable them to be well integrated young adults as well as being competitive at the national, sub-regional and global levels. Therefore, Investing in education and skills development for young people should therefore go beyond increasing basic literacy rates to assure dynamic, multifaceted knowledge-building at higher and tertiary levels. This will go a long way in preparing young people for the evolving labour market.

A much advocated and a long lasting remedy for the youth unemployment is entrepreneurial adventure. A government can hire by itself or can also make a suitable environment for the private sector to hire people. According to a study by Manpower group, both direct employment by the public sector, and direct subsidies for private employment, remain models that appeal to many governments because of their immediate and observable impacts; this sort of approach can, however, be prohibitively expensive, and there is controversy about its long-term effects. The promotion of entrepreneurship is increasingly recognized as an important strategy that can leverage the energy of individuals and civil society to expand the creation and supply of jobs. Such programmes are relevant in both the developing and developed world.

As cited by Manpower Group (2018), in pursuit of effective programme strategies, a study by Card, Kluve, and Weber reviewed nearly 200 programme impacts from 1995-2007 and found that strongest impacts on young people came from job search assistance programmes, while training programmes were more effective in the medium than in the short term. More to revelation cited by

Manpower group, the World Bank's Youth Employment Inventory, an accumulating body of research suggests that such relatively cost-effective programmes can have as great, if not greater impact on youth employment than much more expensive public employment or subsidised hiring.

3

Research Methodology

This chapter describes the research design, study population, sampling design and procedure, data collection instruments, data collection procedures and data analysis. It explains various scientific methods that will be use in achieving the study objectives.

3.1 Research Design

This study will use descriptive survey design. The main advantage of this type of design is that it enables the researchers to assess the situation within the study area at the time of the study. A descriptive research design concerned with describing the characteristics of a particular individual or a group. The researcher therefore will use such design to assess educated youth unemployment rate and its socio-economic effect in case of Yeka sub-city, Woreda 08 at Addis Ababa.

In this study, mixed research approach will be employed; it incorporates elements of both qualitative and quantitative approaches for collecting and analyzing both quantitative and qualitative data in a single study. Among the reasons why researchers employ a mixed methods design is to expand an understanding from one method to another, to converge or confirm findings from different data sources (Creswell, 2015).

Mixed method research has many benefits. One of the benefits to this method is the ability to match the purpose of the method to the need in the study. Some have asked whether this approach to research is helpful or beneficial. "We end with the assumption that the combination of methods provides a better understanding than either the quantitative or qualitative method alone," (Creswell, 2015). The advantage of a mixed methods approach is that it balances efficient data collection and analysis with data. The quantitative data quickly and efficiently captures potentially large amounts of data from large groups of people. The qualitative data provides the appropriate information and facilitates understanding and interpretation of the quantitative data.

The data will be collected based on the sequential explanatory strategy. It is characterised by collecting the quantitative data followed by the collection of qualitative data. Explanatory sequential mixed methods is one in which the researcher first conducts quantitative research, analyzes the results and then builds on the results to explain them in more detail with qualitative research (Creswell, 2015).

3.2 The Target Population

A population or universe for a study is any group of individuals or institutions which have one or more characteristics in common that are of interest to the researcher (Cooper, 1996). The target of the study was unemployed youth population in Woreda 08, Yeka sub-city in Addis Ababa.

3.3 Sampling Method and Technique

Since the study population was heterogeneous stratified sampling was used to divide the sample population into two depending on their sex. Then the total sample size was allocated proportionally equal to the size of the stratum by simple random or lottery sampling method to select youths as respondents. Besides this, purposive sampling technique was used to select Woreda and Yeka sub-city employment concerned officials. Because purposive sampling technique considered as an appropriate sampling technique for the study as it allows only those who were a part of the problem and those who were perceived to have specific information required for the study to participate.

3.4 Sampling Size

The researcher observed the document of the under studied Woreda Administration of Micro and Small Enterprises Offices. According to the data that the researcher gained on the budgetary year, 2012 (2020 G.C) 1,028 youth job seekers were registered and only 82 (7.9 percent) jobs were created. Thus, the researcher took 946 unemployed youths as a total population.

Therefore, in order to determine the sample size of the population, the study used Yamane's (1967) formula with 95 percent confidence and 5 percent acceptable sampling error. Based on the following formula 281 employees were taken as a sample for questionnaire.

n = N, Where, n= is the required sample size

$1 + N \times (e)^2$ N= is the population size

e = the acceptable sampling error (Yamane Taro, 1967).

3.5 Data Collection Methods

The study employed descriptive survey techniques of data collection. It must be noted that the questionnaire survey was used as main data collection instrument of this study because the questionnaire survey enables researchers to examine the socio economic effect of unemployed youths.

3.5.1 Data sources and methods of data collection

The data source for this study was including both primary and secondary sources. Primary data was collected through questionnaire and interview. Close and open ended questionnaires principles of such as, use simple and clear languages, statements should not be too long and use of appropriate punctuations is also considered when developing the instrument. In addition, interviews can be taken as an instrument to strengthen the results of the investigation.

3.5.2 Design of the Instruments

The study employed two kinds of instruments: The questionnaires and interview schedule. The questionnaires consisted of two sections. Section one deals with the demographic variables and other personal information about the respondents. There are a total of 15 items under this section. Section two contains a total of 27 questions that measure the opinion of the respondents related to self-employment and its determinant factors. The second section of the survey questionnaires was focuson cause, socio-economic effects unemployed youths. Items of questionnaire analyzed and rated based on Likert- scale ranging from Strongly Disagree (SD) =1 to Strongly Agree (SA)=5, the questionnaire was developed by the researcher. Its design was based on conceptualisation obtained from the review literature.

3.5.3 Instrument Reliability

The reliability of instruments measures the consistency of instruments. Creswell (2015:190-92) considers the reliability of instruments as the degree of consistency that the instruments or procedure demonstration.

In this study each question rated on a 5-point of Likert response scale which includes strongly disagree (= 1), disagree (= 2), neutral (= 3), agree (= 4) and strongly disagree (= 5)

Based on this internal consistency reliability test was conducted in sample areas, as 21 unemployed youths participated that were included in the actual data and the reliability coefficient of the researcher for the instrument was founded 0.804 which is reliable.

Typically an alpha value of 0.80 or higher was taken as a good indication of reliability. Although other researchers suggests that it is acceptable if it is 0.67 or above (Cohental, 2015: 506). Since instruments were developed based on research questions and objectives; it is possible to collect necessary data from respondents. Then, instruments are consistent with the objectives of the study.

3.5.4 Instrument Validity

A pilot study was conducted to refine the methodology and test instrument such as a questionnaire before administering the final phase. Questionnaires was tested on potential respondents to make the data collecting instruments objective, relevant, suitable to the problem and reliable as recommended by John Adams et al. (2017:136). Issues raised by respondents were corrected and 3 questionnaires were refined. Besides, proper detection by an advisor was also taken to ensure validity of the instruments. Finally, the improved version of the questionnaires were printed, duplicated and dispatched.

The selected instrument can help to assess the cause and the socio-economic effect unemployed youths. The relevant data was collected on the cause and the socio-economic effect unemployed youths through structured interviews can also validate the measurement.

3.5.5 Interviews

After analyzing the data from questionnaires, the researcher went to Woreda 08 and Yeka sub-city employment concerned officials to understand better on few issues in the title of the study. The data for this study was obtained through key-informant interviews are interview with people who know what is going on the socio-economic effect of educated unemployed youth employment.

Purposive sampling technique was used to collect data from the Woreda and Yeka sub-city employment concerned officials. The interviews were conducted with two heterogeneous groups sessions by taking notes up on will of the interviewees, each interview take 30 minutes and a total of 3 hours and 50 minutes spent. The challenges that faced the researcher during interview were time constraint of interviewees because they serve customers each time and each day. Nevertheless, the problem was tackled by discussing with them and they give me their appropriate time.

3.6 Methods of Data Analysis

Descriptive statistics analysis employed to analysis data that are collected from primary source by descriptive survey and the data obtained using interview were organised in tabular form and then carefully analyzed. Descriptive analysis was used to reduce the data in to a summary format by tabulation (the data arranged in a table format) and measure of Likert scale through bar graph, table and descriptive ways in statement. Secondary data being the quantitative information were observed on the current status of educated unemployed youths under study, job creation data by MSEs critically seen to reduce personal biases.

4

Data Analysis and Interpretation

In this chapter the researcher describe and analyze the main variables that associate (or not) with youth unemployment. According to this study, the variables under analysis fit the following dimensions: The demographic traits (age, educational level, and marital status), the cause and the socio-economic effect of youths unemployment.

Descriptive statistics are employed to analyze the primary and secondary data by, frequency, rank and percentile, and hypothesis was tested by using Z- test. The statistics presented are calculated taking into account the weights of each observation and are, therefore, estimates for the sample population.

Table 4.1: Questionnaires Respondents and their Demography Characteristics

		Frequency	Percentage
Questionnaires	Distributed	281	100
	Returned	281	100
Sex	Female	160	47
	Male	121	53
	Total	281	100

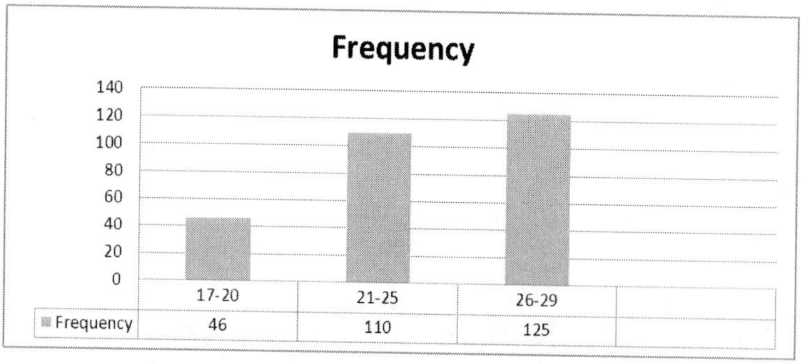

Fig. 4.1: Age distribution of Respondents.

Source: Survey data, 2012 E.C.

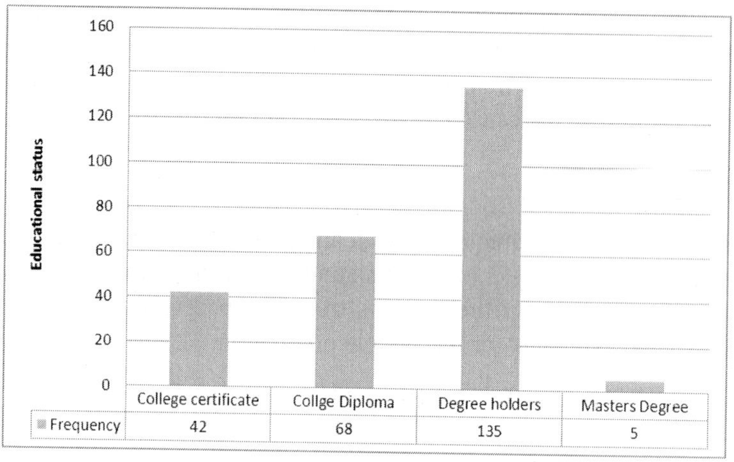

Figure 4.2. Educational status of respondents.

Source: Survey data, 2012 E.C.

4.1 Migration Status of the Respondents

Based on the data shown on Fig. 4.1, 81 percent of the total respondents are resident of this city while the rest 19 percent are migrated from different areas of the country. This data show us there is rural urban migration of educated youth from rural area of the country for searching of better job. Beside migration most youths that are not resident but completed their education in this city most probable youths don't wants to return to their place of residence rather they stayed and searching for an available jobs.

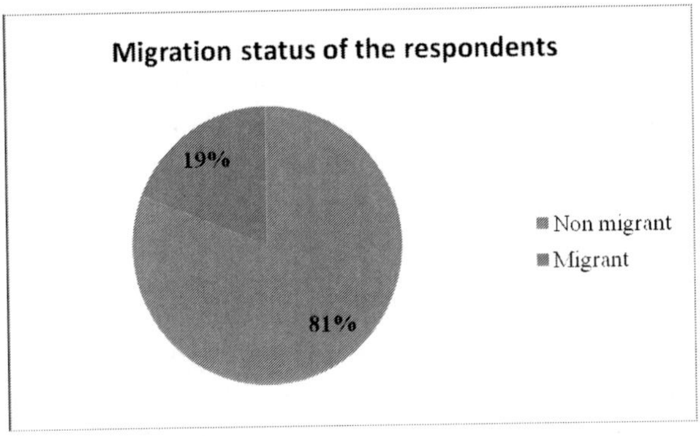

Fig. 4.3: Percentage distribution of migration status of the respondents.

Source: Survey data, 2012 E.C.

4.2 The Main Cause of Educated Youth Unemployment

Although youth unemployment is a major problem in all over the world, the cause of this problem is different from country to country based on the nature and economy of the countries. Here in Ethiopia the cause of youth unemployment is different from area to area in terms of the economic activities of the areas. The causes

Table 4.2: Frequency Distribution of Respondents on the main cause of educated Youth Unemployment

The main causes of educated youth unemployment	SD	%	DA	%	N	%	A	%	SA	%
Quality of education	93	33	86	30.6	3	.06	54	19.2	45	16
Poor entrepreneurship skills	26	9.3	45	16	-	0	124	44.1	86	30.6
Mismatch between training and labor market	10	3.6	17	6	-	0	124	44.1	130	46.2
Poor economy of the country	65	23.1	98	34.9	-	0	72	25.6	46	16.3
Population growth	43	15.3	72	25.6	-	0	108	38.4	58	20.6
State failure to create adequate job	11	3.9	17	6	-	0	109	38.8	144	51.2

Source: Survey data 2012 E.C.

of youth unemployment are also differing based on the educational level of the youth, i.e. low level of education is mentioned as main causes of unemployment for those that are not educated but it could not be a cause for educated youth. Table 4.2 shows the causes of educated youth unemployment based on the nature of the country in the study area.

There are number of causes of educated youth unemployment. The most significant is poor macroeconomic performance of the country in which the absorption capacity of the country's economy for those educated youth is very low (Brousser and Tekilesilassie, 2016). On the other hand, Yohanes and Misaye (2018) in their studies identified that favouritism, corruption, bias and discrimination in different forms played a great role as factors responsible for youth graduates unemployment. The views of the respondent on the main cause of educated youth unemployment in the study area as the above table shown.

4.2.1 Quality of Education

Quality education is crucial for the country's economy and development. Even if most agencies, including government blame the quality of education for the current educated youth unemployment. Majority of the respondents, 33 percent of the total respondents strongly disagree that the quality of education could be the cause to the current educated unemployment problem. Next to this 30.6 percent of respondents also do not believe that quality education could be the cause of educated unemployment youth. While the rest 19.2 percent and 16 percent or respondents agree and strongly agree respectively that quality of education has contribution to educated youth unemployment.

4.2.2 Poor Entrepreneurship Skills

One of the causes of educated youth unemployment is poor entrepreneurship skills. According to Table 4.2, 44.1 percent and 30.6 percent of major respondents agree and strongly agree that poor entrepreneurship skills contributed for educated unemployment youths under study. On the other hand, 9.3 percent and 16 percent study participants replied as agree and disagree respectively that they do not believe poor entrepreneurship skills can be the cause of educated unemployment youths on the study area.

Although respondents response indicate poor entrepreneurship skills is the main cause for youth unemployment there was no good entrepreneurship training in all educational institution which enables them to create their own business and to be self-employed rather than waiting for the government, this data implies that most of of educated youths have no entrepreneurship skill and training in their school.

4.2.3. Mismatch between Training and Requirements of Jobs

Mismatch of education and training skills with the requirements of the labour market is another important reason for the high level of educated unemployment. According to the data shown on the above table, from the total respondent 44.1 percent and 46.2 percent respondents agree and strongly agree in respective way that mismatch between training and requirement of jobs by the economy is the second major rated causes of educated unemployment. In relation to this, one questionnaires respondent filled his additional supportive idea on the questionnaire paper that "I graduated with Heritage Management from Government University before five years ago. I have been checking many job vacancies almost on daily basis; however I have never come cross any vacancy for history and heritage management until I filled this questionnaire".

This data implies that lack of institutional linkage between training institutions and the labour market can be blamed for the difficulties educated youth facing to enter the labour market. This unmet need for employment was the result of a mismatch between labour supply and demand, which the 19th International Conference of Labour Statisticians called labour underutilisation (ILO, 2016 b). However, 3.6 percent and 6 percent of respondents respectively disagree and strongly disagree that mismatch between training and requirements of jobs, can be the cause to the current educated unemployment problem in the study area. This implies the educated youths should not expected job from the government rather they should be self-employed by the skill they gained from college or universities.

4.2.4 Economic Status of the Country

Poor economy is a major problem for most developing countries such as Ethiopia. It is also believed that the main cause of educated unemployment. According to the data shown on Table 4.2, majority respondents comprising with, 23.1 percent and 34.9 percent do not believe that poor economic status of the country as the cause of educated youth unemployment. This implies that Ethiopia has sufficient asset capital to create job opportunity for all her educated youths rather the political atmosphere like ethnic bias, absence of accountability, generally lack of good governance that currently existed in the country created unemployment of youths with a great rate of increment from time to time. However, the government announced and declared the economy of the country has been growing with the double digit economic growth since the last few years but the economy of the country do not assured the inclusive benefit of youths like creating job opportunity for educated youths though they are a pillar for the growth of one's country. Thus, government declaration double digit economic growth of the country remain on report paper as it segregate youths from beneficiary of their countries assets. While the other respondents holding with 25.6 percent and 16.3 percent replies agree and strongly agree that even if the government declared Ethiopia belongs to the fastest growing country still the country is poor to create job opportunity for her all educated youths. In relation to this, Brouser and Teklessilassie (2016) stated that when the economy of the country is poor the labour demand will be low and unable to keep pace with the increases in educational attainment, particular with jobs which demand highly skilled labour. This creates the problem of educated unemployment.

4.2.5 State Failure to Create Adequate Jobs

In many developing countries including Ethiopia the failure of the state in creating jobs and absorbing the existed human recourses is mentioned as a cause for youth unemployment. Based on the data shown in Table 4.2, 38.8 percent and 51.2 percent of the total respondents respectively agree and strongly agree that they blamed the failure of the state in creating jobs for their youth unemployment as the first rated cause for their unemployment. A high level of unemployment indicates that the failure of a state to use its labour resources effectively. There may be a number of reasons to the failure of a state to utilise the existed skilled man power. The main reasons to the failure of a state is poor economic performance due to lack of good governance of the country in which it can't be able to absorb the existed labour resources and lack of an appropriate implementation policy and programme on how to utilise the existing man power especially those educated unemployed youths. However, the rest 3.9 percent and 6 percent of study participants replied disagree and strongly disagree that the state failure can be causes of educated youth unemployment.

4.2.6 Population Pressure

Rapid growth of population is another factor affecting access of job opportunities. The data as shown in Table 4.2, from the total respondents holding with 38.4 percent and 20.6 percent agree and strongly agree respectively that rapid population pressure comes from under study area and rural-urban migration is a contribution factor for the current problem of educated unemployment. While the rest 15.3 percent and 25.6 percent of respondents replied disagree and strongly disagree that population growth as the cause for educated unemployment size of the labour force has been increasing at an average annual rate of 3.2 percent, reached an estimated 32.2 million people while the demand for labour has slower growth rate than the growing population (Nebil *et al.*, 2016).

4.3 Factors that Contribute to the Educated Youth Unemployment

Although there are limited available jobs, most educated youth remains unemployed as a result of several factors. These factors aggravated unemployment rate of educated youth. In the case of Ethiopia, particularly in Addis Ababa, which includes the study area, several factors could contribute to the causes of educated youth unemployment the following are identified as the major factors that make educated youth to stay unemployed while there were job opportunities.

Table 4.3: Factors that Contribute to the educated youth Unemployment

Variable factors	SD	%	DA	%	N	%	A	%	SA	%
Rural-urban migration	25	8.9	32	11.38	-	0	95	33.8	129	45.9
Job selection	64	22.8	45	16	-	0	86	30.6	86	30.6
Lack of work experience	8	2.8	19	6.8	-	0	120	42.7	134	47.7

Source: Survey data 2012 E.C.

4.3.1 Rural Urban Migration

Unemployment is most severe in the urban areas of Ethiopia due to rural-urban migration (Nebil *et al.* 2016). The data shown in the above table revealed this. Out of 281 total respondents majority 129 (45.9 percent) and 95 (33.8 percent) of respondents respectively agree and strongly agree that rural to urban migration is a major contributing factor on the study area for educated youth unemployment. This data implies that there are a large number of educated youth migrants from different areas of the country after they got their TVET certificate, diploma or degree in searching of better job. As a result it makes scrambling and raises competition for limited available jobs. Addis Ababa as the primate city where major cultural, economic and political institutions are situated, it attracts more labour forces from different corner of the country that raises competition and scrambling for limited available jobs. Therefore, this large number of migration of educated youths from different corner of the country makes the unemployment situation of the city very worse. Besides, this implies that how far difficulty in acquiring job opportunity out of Addis Ababa. This might be the major reason that dozens of educated youths displaced their area and migrated towards the capital of the country.

On the other hand, 32 (11.38 percent) and 25 (8.9 percent) study participants disagree and strongly disagree in respective order that rural to urban migration can be the cause of educated youth unemployment that has been really observed in the study area.

4.3.2 Job Selection

Educated youth, most of the time, prefer to be employed in the formal sector rather than engaging in self-employment in informal sector (Serneels, 2017). The response shown in table, from the total respondents two groups of 80 equally rated with (30.6 percent) were found under agree and strongly agree that they had job selection attitude. According to them they refused available jobs because of job selectivity. This information revealed that most of educated youth are highly aspire to get white-collar jobs rather than to be engaged in blue-collar jobs. According to Serneels (2017), for most of educated youth public sector and formal private sector employment are considered 'good jobs' due to their high wages, while self-employment, casual and cooperative employment are considered to be 'bad jobs'. Even though the government media claims that much has been done with the young people's attitude towards available jobs, the response of relatively better educated youth indicated that they are unemployed because they perceived that these (blue-collar) jobs are not meant for them. In addition to closed ended questions the researchers also employed open ended questions. Like the reason why they refused available jobs. Based on their response much of the respondent perceived that going to colleges and universities wouldn't have been necessary to do menial jobs. One respondent wrote this ..."If I knew that my final destination is working in the cobblestone project, I wouldn't have gone to university spending three years to study sociology; three months training and less was enough to have this type of job". However, the other 64 (22.8 percent) and 45(16 percent) of respondents strongly agree and disagree that they had not job selection or job preference mind rather they minded that they do any job because of "something is better than nothing". But currently the chance to do any job is rare due to ethnic bias and stereotypes not only in private sector even in governmental institution. This situation worsening by far to acquire job opportunity for educated unemployed youths.

4.3.3 Lack of Work Experience

Lack of work experience also has many responses from the respondents. The above Table 4.3, almost all respondents, 134 (47.7 percent) and 120 (42.7 percent) shows on their respective response, strongly agree and agree that lack of work experience is a major challenge for them to be hired even in a limited job availability regarding to the number of educated youth job finder. This information implies that most of the vacancies announced both by the private organisation and governmental organisation required even high work experience that extremely lacks fresh graduated youths. Even though the government stated that it creates different jobs in its organisation considering of fresh graduates, in reality they are still suffering from unemployment because of lack of work experience. Therefore, on this situation where there is work experience requirement almost in all organisation including government vacancies make fresh graduates stay unemployed till they find a job that doesn't require work experience. However, the small number, 19 (6.8 percent) and 8 (2.8 percent) opposes that working experience not the working experience rather ethnic stereotypes and lack of transparency and accountability to fairly compete affected them for job hiring.

4.4 Unemployed Educated Youth and Micro Small Scale Enterprises (MSEs)

Since the last few years the government of Ethiopia has been taking measure to reduce problem of youth unemployment. During the two successive developments plans PASDEP (2005/06- 2009/10) and (2010/11-2014/15), more emphasis has been given for Micro and Small Scale Enterprises (MSEs) development based on their potential to create employment opportunities. According to the government report since the establishment, this sector is creating employment for millions of unemployed youth. Although this sectors creates opportunities for most unemployed youths to start their own business and to generate income, the participation of educated youth especially university graduates in this sectors is very low.

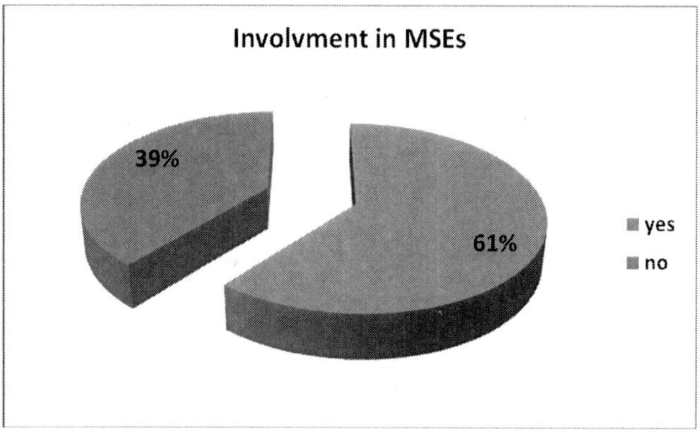

Fig. 4.4: Percentage distribution of the respondent on the involvement of MSEs.

Source: Survey data, 2012 E.C.

The involvement of educated unemployed youth in MSEs as shown on Figure 4.4, most of the respondents, 61 percent said that they were looking for MSEs in searching of jobs while the rest 39 percent of the respondents did not search other jobs. Even though MSEs are thought as a good job creator sectors for unemployed youth, according to them (61 percent of the respondent who were looking for the job in MSEs) no one of the respondent could get job opportunity from this sector. In addition to this the researcher asked those 61 percent respondents who said they were looking MSEs to get employment the reason why they couldn't find job opportunities in this sector. Based on the data which is shown below in Table 4.4, 156 (55.5 percent) and 106 (37.8 percent) of the respondent said corruption is a major problem followed by bureaucracy (36.7 percent=Strongly Agree and 42.3 percent=Agree) not to get job opportunities in MSEs. Thirdly, (22 percent=Strongly Agree and 27.8 percent Agree) saying that there is no job related with their profession in MSEs. In addition to this the researcher observed there is a political based discrimination as a challenge for educated youths to get job opportunities from this sector. However, 22.8 percent (Strongly disagree) and 25.6 percent (disagree) opposes that there is a job related with one's profession in MSEs but the problem unfairness to address all educated youth unemployed under the study area.

Table 4.4: Distribution of respondents on the reason why they couldn't get job in MSEs

Reason not to get job in MSEs	SD	%	DA	%	N	%	A	%	SA	%
Bureaucracy	36	12.8	21	7.4	2	0.7	119	42.3	103	36.7
Corruption	7	2.5	12	4.27	-	0	156	55.5	106	37.8
No job related with your profession	64	22.8	72	25.6	5	1.8	78	27.8	62	22

Source: Survey data, 2012 E.C.

From this finding of the research it can be seen that corruption and bureaucracy are identified as a major problem for educated youth to get job opportunities in MSEs. In addition to this the researcher also observed political based discrimination to enter in these sectors as a problem.

4.5 The Effect of Educated youth Unemployment

Unemployment has multiple economic, psychological, political and environmental consequences on youths. The effects of unemployment can be classified broadly as private (individual) and social effects. The private effects of unemployment are those effects borne by the unemployed youths themselves. The social effects on the other hand refer to those impacts to the societies as well as the nation at large and it can be the cumulative results of private effect (Abebe, 2016). Unemployment effect was dominant among persons who are 21-29 years of age, in which most of them have completed their education and entering to the labour market with no prior work experience (Tesfaye, 2016). Youth unemployment also affect once country economy as a result of wasting of economic resources of productive labour forces and there by affect the long run growth potential of the economy. Unemployment also gives rise to increased crime, suicides, poverty rates, alcoholism, drug addictive and prostitution. Unemployment also has indirect effect on once country resources because it comes up with cost (cost of crime prevention) which rather could have been used for other developmental purpose. Unemployed person had negative attitude towards political system than employed ones. The labour market insecurity increase dissatisfaction and youth violate with the existing political system. Cam filed (2011) stated the implication of educated youth unemployment illustrated by the recent events of the 'Arab Spring' (December 2010 onwards) where a protest by Mohamed Bouazizi, an unemployed graduate living in a provincial town in Tunisia burning himself in the street and sparked both similar protests – another unemployed young man from the same town climbed an electricity pole, shouted "no for misery no for unemployment" then touched the wires and electrocuted himself – and a chain of events that brought down governments across the Middle East. Youth are very sensitive for anything to do, if properly supported and guided, give access to work and follow up continuously can create good citizens and young population in the country. According to Tesfaye (2016), many educated youths complain on adequacy of policies and strategies aimed to addressing unemployment, they have doubt on implementation of the programmes to reduced unemployment rate.

4.5.1 Effects of Unemployment on Educated Themselves

Unemployment educated youth, those residing in Addis Ababa are vulnerable for different socioeconomic problems such as drug addictive, staying and spent their time on the street without any purpose, engaged in crime activities and being dependent on their families. Figure 4.5 shows the effects of unemployment on educated unemployed youth themselves.

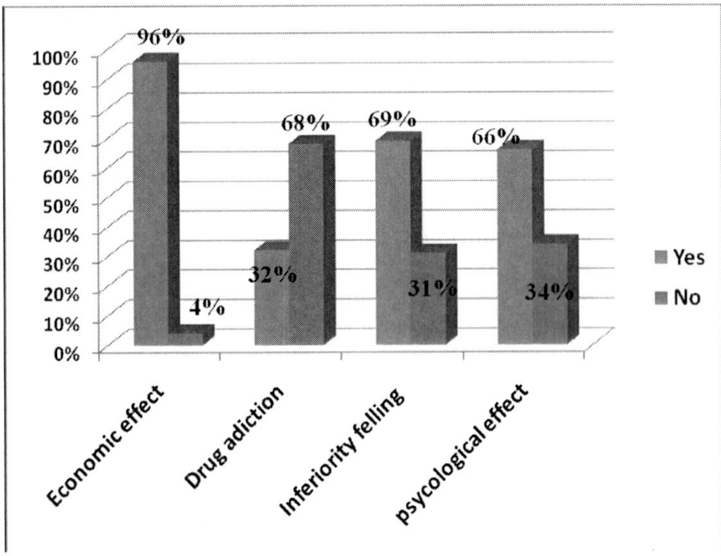

Fig. 4.5: Effects of unemployment on educated youth themselves.

Source: Survey data, 2012 E.C.

Based on the data which is shown in figure 4.5, from the total respondent 96 percent said yes for economic effect whereas inferiority felling and hopelessness had a response of 69 percent from the respondents. The remaining psychological effect and drug addiction had a response of 66 percent and 68 percent respectively. From this information, we can see that economic effect, psychological effect as well as inferiority feeling and hopelessness are the major effect that most of educated youth suffers as a result of unemployment. Educated unemployed are highly affected by lack of income for their livelihoods so that, they couldn't be able to satisfy their basic needs. As a result of this they are trying to cop up from this problem by using different coping mechanisms. According to the respondents some of educated unemployed youth working some menial jobs as they call it in Amharic "tebarari sirawoch" sometimes they also call it "tikakin sirawoch". Some of educated unemployed gathered with their friends and advertising for home to home tutorial service to get an income to cover their expenses while they were looking for formal jobs. Some of educated unemployed youth are stayed at home and economically depended on their family, relatives and friends to cover their basic needs. Most of the informants of the study mentioned that they do not afford to go out to the cafeteria, cinema, and theater with their friends. So that, they have felt that they are socially isolated. According to the informants, they also ashamed themselves because they depended on their families while they expected to support them and they believed that they don't equally participate in the family's and community affairs, and they are not important as long as they have nothing to contribute to their families and communities.

As the informants, unemployed youth with no income also faced the difficulties where to spend their time, spending their time is depended on their, family, friends and relatives economic status and their gender. Unemployed youth from poor families did not have more options in which they can engage to pass their free time. Because many places and options where youth can spend their free time such as watching cinema and theater, playing games, passing time in the cafeteria with their friends and using social media such as internet usually incur costs which is unaffordable for most of them. Consequently, they are more likely suffered from depression, loneliness and mental stresses (Kielbach and Traiser, 2014). Therefore, as Paul and Moser (2015) revealed unemployment have stronger negative psychological and mental effects on people of lower social status. As a result of these most unemployed youths tried to escape from their depression, loneliness and mental stress by using addictive drugs (k'hat,shisha) and different Alcohols.

In addition to this with informal communication with friends and other peoples, the researcher observed that illegal migration is the consequence of unemployment. Even though the government blamed that human trafficker and lack of awareness creation by different stakeholders as a root cause of youth illegal migration, and most people's indicated unavailability of employment opportunities as a cause for illegal out migration. Although the government captured and accused many human traffickers and different Medias including social media trying to aware how dangerous illegal migration is but youth illegal out migration is still highly continues. In relation to this one informant say this in Amharic "be endezih ayinet huneta ezih hager keminor yilk ye qey bahir shark bibelagn emertalehu". "For me, it is better to be eaten by red sea sharks than living in this country in such situation". Therefore, even though it's much known how illegal migration is dangerous for most people and even for them, unemployment forced them to be illegally migrated by the hope of getting better job with scarification of their lives and most of the youths lost their live on the way of this illegal migration (i.e. slaughtered of 30 Ethiopian youths by ISIS militant last year, and last month boat sank in Mediterranean sea on the way from Egypt to Europe where more than 500 peoples diad. There were Ethiopians among those who diad in the sea as reported by different social medias).

4.5.2 Effects of Educated Unemployment on the Societies

Educated youth unemployment doesn't only affect unemployed themselves but rather it affects their family and the society at large. According to Abebe (2016), societies are affected by the total cumulative effects of individuals who are affected by unemployment. Therefore, there is economic as well as social effect on the community as a result of educated youth unemployment.

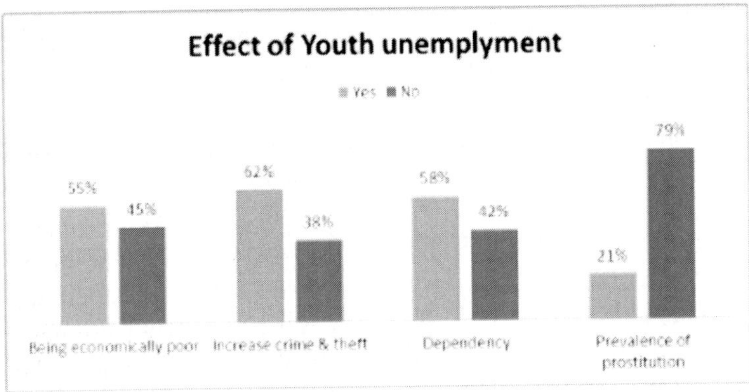

Fig. 4.6: Effects of educated unemployment on their family and on the societies

Source: Survey data, 2012 E.C.

Based on the response on Table 4.6, poverty has the response of 55 percent, on the other hand rising of theft and other crime has got 62 percent whereas dependency got a response of 58 percent and prevalence of prostitution got 21 percent response especially on girls. As we can see from this information, poverty, dependency, and the rising of theft and other crimes often affect the society as a result of unemployment of educated youth. Most of unemployed youth have no means of income for their day to day expense and remain dependent on their families, relatives as well as on their friends. Obviously it's very common in Ethiopia that family has a significant role to play in supporting young people financially, socially and psychologically when they are unemployed. The family continues to support their young ones as much as they can up until they are able to secure any means of survival. Families do this because there is no any other means such as social security or other unemployment benefits. According to the information obtained through informal communication, in the family the older son or daughter who already had a job may share the burden of supporting the younger ones in their course of transition from school to work. All this in sum increase the prevalence of poverty in their family as well as in the society at large.

Educated youth with no employment where their parents and relatives couldn't afford to support them and have no one in supporting their financial and material needs may tend to do theft and commit other crimes as a means of coping up their financial need this is highly affect the day to day activities of the society as well as peace and security of the society. Sometimes youth women's who have no job and have no means of income may tend to do prostitution to get an income as a result it increases the prevalence of HIV/AIDS. As Abebe (2016), unemployment of youths considered as a risk factor for the distribution of HIV/AIDS. In addition to this the researcher asked the effects of educated youth unemployment on the generation. Most of the informants replied that educated youth unemployment has an advert effect on young generation's attitude towards education. Most youngsters are hoping to live a better life through education and investing their scarce resource on schooling. But when they see their elders in unemployment even though they are educated, and know that education is not the only way to improve their livelihood and to lead a better life, their aspiration to attend their education will be decreased. Now-a-days there is a statement that is said by most of youngsters in Amharic "Yetemarena ye bela wodko aywodikim yemibalew dro kere yilk timihrtna daget eyarefu new". Those who educated and those who eat most never remained failed does not work this time. Rather, education and mountain climbing is better with rest in relation to this one interviewee said this … "Of course I believe in education, everybody must do at least secondary education, in my opinion university education is important as far as it gives you job otherwise, I consider it as wasting time". Beside social and individual effect youth unemployment may also has a political consequence because most unemployment youth especially those educated unemployed youth blamed the government and its policy for the cause of their unemployment. As a result they have negative attitude and dissatisfaction with the existing political system (Camfield, 2011; Tesfaye, 2016).

Table 4.5: Educated Unemployed Youths Registered Data and performance of the study area (2014-2018 E.C.)

	Data of MSE							
	Registered Job seeker			Job created for job seeker Youths			Performance against plan (%)	Performance report to Yeka sub –city (%)
	M	F	T	M	F	T		
2014	432	198	630	124	18	142	22.5	40.5
2015	504	156	660	89	29	118	17.8	34.8
2016	628	194	822	128	28	156	18.9	32.2
2017	729	208	937	85	39	124	13.2	25.6
2018	650	374	1024	71	11	82	8	20.9
Total	**2943**	**1130**	**4027**	**497**	**125**	**622**	15.44	

Source: Compiled from Yeka sub-city, Woreda 08 MSE (2018).

From the above data, we can understand that, except the budgeted year 2018 job seeker educated unemployed youths increases but the job created according to the plan is very poor. It declines from the period onwards especially in the 2018 budgeted year.

Surprisingly, but deliberately the Woreda concerned MSEs officer made a double lie and falsified performance report to his respective Yeka sub-city MSEs head office since 2014-2018 in the above Table as a researcher examines the strategic plan of job creation given to the Woreda and cross-check the real performance of job creation of the Woreda and the report made to the sub-city.

Anyway, this poor performance and falsified report of creating job for educated unemployed youths is because of the following reason as the data gained from interview informant's of the sub-city and Woreda MSEs officers. They raised the following reasons for poor implementation of job creation and lie report.

(i) Weak institutional capacity and systems: The employment service centers lack even the basic institutional capacity to provide the basic employment services. There are very weak institutional systems and manuals that guide the identification and registration of vacancies, establishment of collaborations with potential employers, and transparent screening and matching of job seekers with available job opportunities. In light of their limited institutional capacity, potential employers including public bodies lack confidence in the services provided by public employment service centers. As a result, potential employers tend to advertise their job openings through mass media rather than using the services of public employment agencies. Private firms also prefer to use private employment agencies for a fee rather than public employment service centers that offer their services free of charge.

(ii) **Limited Use of Information Technology:** The employment services lacks systematised and automated processes to fulfill their job-matching role efficiently. There is limited use of information technology to support the provision of employment services. There is no electronic database and data exchange platform to facilitate job matching between employers and job seekers. PES centers receive announcements of job vacancies from firms, and CVs from job seekers via personal visits. Thus, neither firms nor job seekers have access to the existing paper-based jobseeker and vacancy registration records, resulting in the few staff being solely responsible for matching vacancies with jobseekers, selecting jobseekers and forwarding their CVs to the firms. The use of manual system did not only make the provision of employment services inaccessible to both job seekers and employers, it also made job matching very difficult for staff. The lack of automated and systematised processes also results in unsystematic follow-up on the recruitment of jobseekers by prospective employers.

(iii) **Mandate overlap and poor cooperation and collaboration among different public employment service providing agencies:** Different organisations are involved in the provision of employment services, including labour and social affairs offices, MSEDAs, youth and sports and others. These offices, however, don't work closely and collaboratively in registration of job seekers, identification of vacancies and placement activities. They often act independently. Much resource could have been saved if they collaborate in job seeker registration and provision of other employment services.

(iv) **Poor visibility:** Employment services are not promoted to job seekers and potential employers to use their services. According to key informants, the general public is unaware of the employment services provided by public employment service centers as they don't engage in building relationships and promoting their services.

(v) **Lack of necessary resource:** Employment services are under resourced, according to many key informants. Employment creation using public employment agencies particularly through labour and social services are given very minimal attention. The government rather gave due attention to MSEDAs that support job seekers to engage in self-employment opportunities. The allocated budget at all levels for public employment services in most cases is too small to provide some of the basic employment services. Supportive supervision of Woreda's and sub-city administration labour and social affairs offices due to unavailability of budget. As a result, they chose to just receive reports from lower level government bodies. They believe that they could have improved employment services that the Woreda provide adequate support to the employment service centers.

(vi) **Lack of adequate and qualified staff:** Most, if not all, public employment service centers are understaffed. They also lack qualified staff to provide the required employment services. To many key informants, the salary scale for staff involved in employment service provision is even lower than the one that is being paid to staff with similar qualification in other government agencies. As a result, people that were demoted due to their poor performance in other government agencies are often relegated and assigned to public employment service centers. The unattractive salary paid to public employment service staffs often cause high turnover. The consultant also observed the assignment of newly recruited staff in many places owing to the high staff turnover. Staff also lacks even the basic skills they need to search for vacancies, and provide job search assistance, placement services and counseling services. They also lack sufficient knowledge on other alternative employment services.

(vii) **Voluntary nature of job seeker and vacancy registration:** Registration of job seekers and vacancies is voluntary. There is no legal framework that forces employers to register their vacancies. Coupled with their lack of visibility and poor institutional capacity, very few organisations notify their job openings to public employment agencies. To make matters worse, public employment agencies lack capacity and resources to establish contacts and collaborative relationships with potential employers so as to get vacancy notifications and ensure that their services are used by employers. Their poor track record in facilitating placement services is also serving as a disincentive for job seekers to use their services. Both public and private employment agencies don't also cooperate to notify job openings. Those that do notify their vacancies also announce their vacancies with other media which reduces the chances of getting the vacant positions. As a result, the number of job seekers and vacancies registered in Ethiopia may not reflect the reality on the ground.

(viii) **Poor monitoring and evaluation systems:** Employment service centers don't have proper systems to regularly monitor their performance and evaluate their overall effectiveness in the provision of their services. They don't even have a system and practice that they use to check whether the short listed job seekers sent to employers were actually employed or not. In the absence of such systems and strong monitoring from higher level agencies, the public employment service centers report all the job seekers sent to employers following a job opening notification as employed.

(ix) **Limited government support:** Much of the weaknesses and challenges identified above such as understaffing and poor institutional capacity are related to the inadequate attention given to public employment services by the government. Job creation through labour and social affairs offices is often seen as secondary. A key informant from one center was quoted as saying "Compared to the support provided to the city MSEDA, the sub-city administration provides no support to the labour and social affairs office." MSEDA staff and officials, on their part, attributed the limited attention given to labour and social affairs offices to their poor performance in placement and job creation. They argue that labour and social affairs offices are there to collect and report what they (MSEDAs) have done rather than engaging in facilitating employment and creating job opportunities for job seekers. According to them, the government's increased attention to MSEDAs was due to their noticeable contribution to significant job creation and economic development in the country which has not been the case at labour and social affairs offices. However, the target groups to MSEDAs are often youth and women that are willing to engage in self-employment opportunities. Labour and social affairs offices have significant roles in at least promoting employment services for people that are not targeted by MSEDAs. Besides, MSEDAs seem to have misunderstood the role and mandate of PESOs as they expect them to create jobs like them.

(x) Limited absorptive capacity of the economy: Different documented evidences argue that the Ethiopian economy has limited capacity to absorb the ever increasing labour force. The limited number of employer organisations available in the country was also cited as a big challenge by some public employment service centers to find job opportunities for job seekers. Even so, public employment service staff in most centers seems to be under the impression that the lack of will from employers to notify their vacancies is a major challenge to increase their placement services.

4.6 Possible Strategy to Alleviate Educated Youth Unemployment

There are possible ways to solve educated youth unemployment problems through the participation and intervention of different stakeholders. Even if the government is expected as major actors in reducing the existed educated unemployment problem, educated youth themselves, families, societies and different social organisation also should have a responsibility in fighting this problem in the study area negative attitude and dissatisfaction with the existing political system (Camfield, 2011; Tesfaye, 2016).

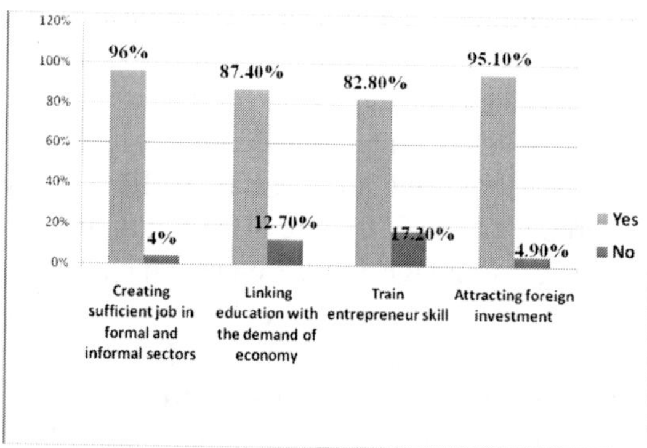

Fig. 4.7: Possible solution to reduce educated youth unemployment in the study area.

Source: Survey data, 2012 E.C.

According to the information on Figure 4.7, creating sufficient jobs had a response of 96 percent of the total respondents. Attracting foreign investment has a response of 95.1 percent. Linking education with the demand of the economy had 87.4 percent of the total respondent whereas encouraging foreign investment has got a response of 82.8 percent. According to the information on the above graph, the highest respondent mention to fight educated youth unemployment problem are creating sufficient jobs in both formal and informal sectors. Even though the government made effort in reducing youth unemployment through the expansion of Micro and small scale enterprises but it's not considering educated youth. The researcher observed from the respondents, most of educated youth do not want to work as a day labourer in housing and construction works or may not willing to work in cobblestone paving while he/she studied medicine, business and other fields. Rather they want to work similar work with the field that they studied. Therefore, the government should have to create jobs in formal sectors or have to facilitate those informal sectors to be a good working environment for those educated unemployed persons. Attracting labour intensive foreign investment also described as an alternative. Another alternative that was described by most respondents in reducing educated unemployed youth is linking education with the demand of economy. In relation to mismatch between education and demand of the economy, unemployed youth, particularly those with higher education qualifications complained about the irrelevance of some fields of studies offered in universities that are not wanted to the labour market. Most of them believed that schooling is supposed to be responsive to the demand in the labour market. Therefore the government should have to do more on institutional linkage between educational institution and the labour demand. Lack of entrepreneurship skill is cause of youth unemployment. Therefore, to reduce this problem much work should be done in scaling up entrepreneurship skill of the student during their schooling time. Giving entrepreneurships skill as a course may help them to develop their entrepreneurship skill. As a result they could be able to create their own business rather waiting for jobs from the government.

Scaling up entrepreneurships skill of the youth its self may not be a solution but in addition to this enhancing credit provision and other encouragement is needed. Another option in fighting for reducing youth unemployment is controlling of rapid population growth and reducing high flow of young people from countryside to the city by creating work opportunity in their place of residence so this all need to take immediate action as a solution.

In addition to these, the researcher was asked open ended question to the respondents on what is the responsibility of the societies, the families and educated unemployed themselves. According to them the societies and families should have a responsibility to aware the youths and encouraging them to do job without selection. Educated unemployed also have not only waiting for the government for white collar-jobs rather they should work in any job without selection till they find their inspired jobs.

Table 4.6: Percentage Distribution of Respondent on the problems seeking to address in reducing of educated unemployment in the study area

Problems on reducing educated unemployment	SD	%	DA	%	N	%	A	%	SA	%
Lack of commitment of youths	36	12.8	43	15.3	-	0	89	31.7	113	40.2
Corruption	9	3.2	14	5	-	0	149	53	109	38.8
Lack of transparency & Accountability	14	5	22	7.8	-	0	112	39.9	133	47.3

Source: Survey data, 2012 E.C.

According to the data on Table 4.6, of the total respondents, the most rated respondents 149 (53 percent) agreed and 109 (38.8 percent) strongly agreed that corruption is a major problem while lack of transparency and accountability and lack of commitment had strongly agreed response of 47.3 percent and agreed response of 39.9 percent respectively. Based on the finding corruption is identified as a major problem that should be avoided in programmes of reducing educated unemployment. Most of educated unemployed complained that, now-a-day family network is very important to acquire job in all the governmental institutions, and in private and informal sectors. This works through the connections and influences that family and relatives endowed based on their socio-cultural and economic positions in the society. Unemployed youth from well off background as Jeffrey (2018) argues have better "social connections and cultural confidence" than unemployed youth from poor background who usually lack of economic, social and cultural advantage. In addition to corruption the researcher observed from informal communication from different youths that, there is political based discrimination in the study area. Members of ruling political party are more advantageous in recruitment in different governmental organisations than that of not members of the party. Thus, government and administration of the city should have taken measures to address these problems.

Lastly, strongly agreed respondents (40.2 percent) and 31.7 percent agreed respondents replied that lack of commitment by educated youths themselves leads to a problem to reduce educated unemployment in the study area while the rest respondents opposes that we are committed but our effort to commitment bring nothing to reduce unemployment rate in the study area.

5

Conclusion and Recommendations

5.1 Conclusion

As the study revealed in the study area, most of young people are attaining their formal education with the hope of leading a better life and improving their livelihood. As a result those young people's and their families are investing their scarce resource on school education on the aspiration of securing a better job which in turn improving their income and overcome poverty. Although, young people's and their families who placed their hopes on education that is associated with upward social mobility and improvement of livelihoods, most youth in their post schooling life have to face unemployment challenges and remain jobless for an extended period of time.

The increased in the number of students enrollments at all levels with the limited employment creation by the economy brought educated unemployment phenomenon in the country. This has created the gap between young people's expectation of education and the reality they encounter. To this end, as UN (2018) puts "failure to coordinate education provision with labour market needs" has contributed to the excessive educated youth unemployment. The situation has largely affected new labour market entrant young people with hopeful aspirations. For some of these group expectations to lead better life through formal education are not being achieved and dependence on their family has rather been prolonged.

In this study, an attempt has been made to Assessing Youth Unemployment Rate and its effect in case of Yeka sub-city, Woreda 08. Thus, there are several factors identified as the main causes for educated youth unemployment. To mention some of them are poor economic performance of the country, state failure in creating adequate jobs are identified as a cause for educated unemployment. Skill mismatch also identified as a cause of educated youth unemployment. The irrelevance of certain trainings to the labour market demand has witnessed the poor linkage between training institutions and the labour market. The study also identified lack of entrepreneurship skill as a cause for educated youth to be waiting for job from the government, rather than creating their own business. As a result of this educated youth remains unemployed until they found job from government.

The study also tried to explore the factors that make educated youth to be unemployed while there is an available job, according to the study, rural urban migration is indicated as a factor in the study area because it makes scrambling on the limited available jobs. Attitude of job selection also makes educated youth to be unemployed because most of educated youths are highly aspire for white-collar jobs. Young educated people also face difficulties to get jobs due to lack of work experiences. The study looks the involvement of educated youth in informal sectors like MSEs. According to the study even though, most educated youth tried to get opportunity in this sector, they couldn't get engage in this sector yet as a result of several factors. Of these factor, bureaucracy, corruption and works do not relate with their profession are identified as a factor for not to get job opportunity in this sector.

This study also assessed the effect of educated youth unemployment on educated unemployed themselves, on their family and the society as a whole. According to the study, lack of income for their basic need, inferiority feeling, psychological effect and drug addicted mentioned as a major effect on educated youth as a result of unemployment. The problem of educated unemployment also affected unemployed youth families and the societies. Rising theft and crime, increasing dependency, prevailing of poverty and prostitution are indicated as major effects as a result of educated unemployment. An attempt also made to assess the views of educated unemployed youth on the possible strategies to solve this problem. As a result, attracting foreign investment, matching education with labour market, scale up the entrepreneurships skills of the student and creating adequate jobs in both formal and informal sectors are stated as a solution.

5.2 Recommendations

The study identified multitude of factors responsible for high rate of educated youth unemployment in the study area. It can be seen that educated youth unemployment issues in Ethiopia remain a continuing problem until high priorities are given to the situations and addressed accordingly. Therefore, based on the finding of this study, the following recommendations are made.

The head government, sub-city administration and Woreda 08 of Yeka sub-city, in collaboration with other concerned bodies should have to progress the economy and create adequate jobs by attracting labour intensive foreign investment that can create more jobs for educated youths.

The city and sub-city government should work for good governance rather than personal gain.

To reduce the skill mismatch problem, action should be taken in enhancing the responsiveness of education institution to the labour market demands by strengthening the linkage between education institutions and the labour market.

Action should be taken in enhancing the entrepreneurship skill of the student by giving entrepreneurship as one subject in all educational institution and, arrange credit facilities for educated unemployed to create their own business.

To fight educated youth unemployment problem in the city, action should be taken to control high flow of young people from countryside to this city where it has the contribution factor for the prevalence of educated unemployment and it need to take immediate action as a solution by creating job opportunity for migrants in their area.

Lack of work experience is mentioned as a challenge to get hired in different institution, thus, at least governmental vacancies should be consider those fresh graduates.

Micro and Small Enterprises (MSEs) should have consider and participate educated youth especially university graduates in facilitating and creating at least similar jobs with their profession.

One of the challenges that make educated youth to stay unemployed with available job is job selection attitude. Therefore, government, families, societies and all concerned bodies should have to create awareness towards job selection attitudes.

References

Abebe, (2016). The impact of youth unemployment on social aspects, Addis Ababa, Ethiopia.

ACEVO (2017). Youth unemployment: the crisis we cannot afford. Association of Chief Executives of Voluntary Organisations. London, UK.

Addis Ababa City Government, Yeka sub-city, Woreda 08 (2020). Small Scale and Microenterprise Quarterly Report for the Month ending April 30, 2014.Unpublished report. Addis Ababa, Ethiopia.

African Youth Report, Addressing the youth education and employment nexus in the new global economy. ECA, Addis Ababa, Ethiopia.

Agnes, S., Ginette, M., Nawsheen, E., and Joao C., (2013). Accelerating the AfDB's Response to the Youth Unemployment Crisis in Africa. AFDB, African Economic Brief, AEB Volume 4, Number 1.

Anita, S. (2018). Well-being of youth: impact of unemployment. Psychology Department, Volume 2, No. 4, World Science Publisher, United States.

Berhanu Denu, Abraham Tekeste and Hannah V., (2017). Characteristics and determinants of youth unemployment, underemployment and inadequate employment in Ethiopia.

Brousser and Tekilesilassie, (2016). The cause of Youth unemployment, New York, USA.

Blackburn, R., (2016). "Understanding Unemployment: The Need for a Social Perspective. International Journal of Sociology and Social Policy, Vol. 8 Iss: 1, pp.1 – 22 University of Cambridge, MCB UP Ltd Publication, London, UK.

Cohental, (2015: 506). Research reliability, (2rd ed.). Sage, Los Angeles, CA, USA.

Cooper (1996). Research methodologies, Choosing among five approaches (3nd ed.). Sage, Thousand Oaks, CA:

Creswell, J. (2015). Qualitative inquiry and research design: Choosing among five approaches (2nd ed.). Sage, Thousand Oaks, CA.

Creswell, J. (2015). Research design: Qualitative, quantitative, and mixed methods approach. (3rd ed.). Sage. Los Angeles, CA, USA.

CSA (2018). The 2007 Population and Housing Census of Ethiopia. FDRE, Central Statistics Authority. Addis Ababa, Ethiopia.

CSA, (2018). Urban Employment /Unemployment Survey. FDRE, Central Statistics Authority. Addis Ababa, Ethiopia.

ECA (2018). The challenge of African youth population, London, England.

FDRE, (1993/1994). Constitution of Federal Democratic Republic of Ethiopia. Addis Ababa, Ethiopia.

George, K., Kobena, T., Hanson and Frannie, A., (2015). World Journal of Entrepreneurship, Management and Sustainable Development, Vol. 7, Nos. 2/3/4, 2011 Regional Integration Policies to Support Job Creation For Africas Burgeoning Youth Population.

Getinet Astatike, (2015).The incidence of youth unemployment in urban Ethiopia, Lancaster University, UK.

GYD Consulting Plc. (2016). The study of Youth Unemployment and Marginalization in Ethiopia. CCRDA. Addis Ababa, Ethiopia.

ILO, (2016). "Resolution concerning statistics of the economically active population, employment, unemployment, and underemployment, adopted by the Thirteenth International Conference of Labour Statisticians"; Retrieved November 26, 2016.

ILO, Employment Strategy Department. Addis Ababa, Ethiopia. Bernhard H., (2016). Perception in action: multiple roles of sensory information in action control. Marta Olivetti Belardinelli and Springer-Verlag. Rome, Italy.

Jasmine, L., and Marco, G., (2018). Youth Coping with Unemployment: The Role of Social Support. University of Geneva, Switzerland.

John Adams *et al.* (2017:136). Research validity Qualitative research methods for social sciences 4th ed. California State University. Long Beach, USA Catherine P., and Nicholas M., (2006).

Kim, B., Lawrence H. (2014).The Youth Labour Market Problem: Its Nature, Causes, and Consequences. University of Chicago, Chicago, USA.

Lizzie, C., Katy, J., Nye, C., and Jenny, G., (2018). International Lessons: Youth unemployment in the global context. The work foundation publications London, UK. www.theworkfoundation.com

Mafiri, M., (2018). Socio-economic impact of unemployment in South Africa. University of Pretoria (pub). Pretoria, South Africa.

Manpower Group (2015). "Wanted: Energized, Career-Driven Youth," what business can do now http://

www.manpowergroup.com/investors/releasedetail.cfm?ReleaseID=665045

Maria, S., (2016). Labour market flexibility and employment and income security in Ethiopia, Employment Strategy Paper, ILO, Addis Ababa, Ethiopia.

Martha Kibru, (2016). Employment Challenges in Ethiopia. Addis Ababa, Ethiopia.

MoFED (2009). Growth and Transformation Plan. Ministry of Finance and Economic Development (MoFED). Addis Ababa, Ethiopia.

MoLSA (2009). National Youth employment strategy (NEPS). FDRE, MoLSA. Addis Ababa, Strategy of Ethiopia Policy report. Addis Ababa, Ethiopia.

MYSC (2004). National Youth Policy. FDRE, Ministry of Youth, Sports and Culture (MYSC). Addis Ababa, Ethiopia

Nancey, P., and Anthony, M., (2017). Some implications of the psychological experiences of unemployment. Autralian journal of career development volume 18(3). University of Southern Queensland. Toowoomba, Australia.

Nebil Kellow, Gezahegn Ayele, and Hayat Yusuf (2018). Enabling the Private Sector to Contribute to the Reduction of Urban Youth Unemployment in Ethiopia. The Addis Ababa Chamber of Commerce and Sectoral Associations and SIDA, Addis Ababa, Ethiopia.

Neil, L., Paul S., Brhmie B., Katy J., and Nye C. (2018). Short-term crisis - long-term problem? Addressing the youth employment challenge. Lancaster University, the work foundation, UK.

Nzinga, H. and Tsegay Gebrekidan, (2018).Youth Unemployment: Ethiopia, Country Studying. International Growth Center

(IGC) London School of Economics and Political Science, London, UK.

Peter, J. (2018). Essentials of Macroeconomics. Peter Joschumzen and Ventus Publishing Aps. Lund, Sweden.

Pieter, S. (2018).Unemployment duration, job search and labour market segmentation Evidence from urban Ethiopia, University of East Anglia. Contact: p.serneels@uea.ac.uk

Serneels (2017), *Youth work attitudes, Moscow, Russia.*

Taye Assefa, (2018). Digest of Ethiopia's National Policies, Strategies and Programs, Forum for Social Studies (FSS). Addis Ababa, Ethiopia.

Tesfaye, (2016). Challenges of youths unemployment in Ethiopia, Addis Ababa, Ethiopia.

Yamane's (1967). Sample population determination, Addis Ababa, Ethiopia.

Yohanes and Misaye (2018). *Cause of youth unemployment, good governance,* Addis Ababa, Ethiopia.

UN (2018). World Youth Report. United Nations, New York, USA.

UN DESA, Department of Economic and Social Affairs (2017). Assessing National Youth Policies in Africa: Five country experiences. Workshop Report – December 2007. Addis Ababa, Ethiopia.

UNDP (2016). The impact of youth unemployment, New York, USA.

Woldehanna, Hoddinott and Dercon, (2018). Growth of Ethiopia and poverty reduction, Oxford University Press. New York, USA.

World Bank, 2018. Job opportunity in developing countries. London, England.

Index

Q

R

S

T

U

W

Y

Z